Read
YOUR PARTNER
LIKE A BOOK

EVERYTHING YOU SHOULD KNOW...
BUT NEVER THOUGHT TO ASK

ROBERT K. ELDER

RUNNING PRESS
PHILADELPHIA

For Betsy,
my favorite book.

Running Press
Hachette Book Group
1290 Avenue of the Americas,
New York, NY 10104
www.runningpress.com
@Running_Press

Printed in China

First Edition: April 2019

Published by Running Press, an imprint of Perseus Books, LLC, a subsidiary of Hachette Book Group, Inc. The Running Press name and logo is a trademark of the Hachette Book Group.

The Hachette Speakers Bureau provides a wide range of authors for speaking events. To find out more, go to www.hachettespeakersbureau.com or call (866) 376-6591.

The publisher is not responsible for websites (or their content) that are not owned by the publisher.

Print book cover design by Frances Soo Ping Chow. Interior design by Melissa Gerber. Map Illustration copyright © iStock / Getty Images Plus/Oleg Chepurin

Library of Congress Control Number: 2018960845

ISBNs: 978-0-7624-9426-2

1010

10 9 8 7 6 5 4 3 2 1

ACKNOWLEDGMENTS

Thanks to my amazing editor, Jennifer Kasius, for making this project a reality and pushing me to make it better. Special thanks also go out to my superstar agent, David Dunton, who was right about this project from the start and was kind enough not to gloat about how right he was. And is. Thanks so much to you both.

Introduction

DO YOU KNOW WHAT MAKES YOUR PARTNER TICK?
HOW THEY GIVE AND RECEIVE LOVE?
THE THINGS THAT MAKE THEM THE HAPPIEST—OR MOST SCARED?

Or do you just *think* you know?

Read Your Partner Like a Book can help. This journal of questions will help promote open communication and bonding—all while getting to know your partner better. It's a playful, light-hearted approach to some serious business.

Think of it as *The Five Love Languages* meets *The Newlywed Game*. You fill out one part of the book—answering for yourself and guessing at what your partner's answers might be—then flip it over to see how closely your answers match. Or don't match.

But remember: Have fun.

We've adapted techniques from matchmakers, Catholic Pre-Cana lessons, and scientific attachment research, to build a fun, guided tour through your partner's psyche with prompts that can be answered together or separately.

We cover topics such as communication styles, conflict resolution skills, money management, sense of humor, career aspirations, cohabitation, family relationships, and sex. (We've even included a super-secret code word page that you can rip out. It encourages openness, honesty, and a little clandestine naughtiness.)

Think of this as a handbook, as well as an irreverent guide to your beloved's mind and a map to mutual happiness and understanding.

—Robert K. Elder
Chicagoland, 2019

SIDE A

USING ROCK BANDS AS A METAPHOR, IN THIS RELATIONSHIP I'M:

a) The depraved, charismatic lead singer

b) The brooding but brilliant guitar player

c) The booze-fueled, anything-goes drummer

d) The spacey tambourine player

e) The quiet, contemplative bassist who holds everything together

MY PARTNER WOULD SAY:

_____

_____

_____

_____

_____

_____

_____

_____

_____ .

I WOULD GRADE OUR FIRST DATE WITH A: _____.
HERE'S WHY:

_____

_____

_____

_____

_____

_____

_____

MY PARTNER WOULD SAY:

_____

_____

_____

_____

_____

_____

_____

IF IT WEREN'T FOR YOU, I'D BE:

_____

_____

_____

_____

_____

_____

_____ .

- -

IF IT WEREN'T FOR ME, YOU'D BE:

_____

_____

_____

_____

_____

_____

_____ .

THE CELEBRITY I MOST LOOK LIKE IS:

_____

_____.

THE CELEBRITY MY PARTNER LOOKS MOST LIKE:

_____

_____.

THIS MOVIE TITLE DESCRIBES OUR LOVE-MAKING STYLE:

a) *The Fast and the Furious*

b) *True Grit*

c) *Cat on a Hot Tin Roof*

d) *Splendor in the Grass*

e) _____

MY PARTNER WOULD SAY:

_____

_____

_____

_____

_____

_____

_____

_____

_____ .

**If you don't want to be explicit, use code words with an * Then use the super-secret code word page, which can be ripped out for privacy.

I CAN MAKE MY PARTNER LAUGH BY:

_____

_____

_____

_____

_____

_____

_____

_____

MY PARTNER CAN MAKE ME LAUGH BY:

_____

_____

_____

_____

_____

_____

_____

_____

THESE THINGS MAKE ME THE MOST ANXIOUS:

_____

_____

_____

_____

_____

_____

_____

_____

THESE THINGS MAKE MY PARTNER
THE MOST ANXIOUS:

_____

_____

_____

_____

_____

_____

_____

SHOULD MY PARTNER GO TO PRISON, I WOULD WAIT FOR THEM:

a) Until they pass the first gate.

b) 1-2 years

c) 3-5 years

d) 5-10 years

e) A lifetime. Or, until they are shanked in the cafeteria.

IN HIGH SCHOOL, MY CLASSMATES
WOULD DESCRIBE ME AS:

_____

_____

_____ .

BUT NOW I'M:

_____

_____

_____ .

MY PARTNER WOULD SAY:

_____

_____

_____

_____

_____

_____ .

MY FIRST IMPRESSION OF YOU WAS:

_____

_____

_____

_____

_____

_____

_____

_____ .

- -

YOUR FIRST IMPRESSION OF ME WAS:

_____

_____

_____

_____

_____

_____

_____

_____ .

MY FAVORITE OUTFIT IS:

_____

_____

_____ /

BECAUSE:

_____

_____

_____ .

MY PARTNER'S FAVORITE OUTFIT IS:

_____

_____

_____ /

BUT THEY LOOK BEST IN:

_____

_____

_____ .

POLITICALLY, I'M _____.

<--------------------|-------------------->

Extremely Left   Happily Moderate   Hard-core Right

- -

MY PARTNER IS HERE [ARROW TO THE SPECTRUM].

<--------------------|-------------------->

Extremely Left   Happily Moderate   Hard-core Right

MY PERSONAL MOTTO IS:

_____
_____
_____
_____
_____
_____
_____
_____

MY PARTNER'S PERSONAL MOTTO IS:

_____
_____
_____
_____
_____
_____
_____
_____

MY PARTNER IS:

a) A Mama's boy

b) A Daddy's girl

c) An Uncle's wingman

d) The milkman's kid

e) Other: _____

MY FAVORITE THING TO DO ON A ROAD TRIP IS:

_____

_____

_____

_____

_____

_____

_____ .

MY PARTNER'S FAVORITE THING TO DO
ON A ROAD TRIP IS:

_____

_____

_____

_____

_____

_____

_____

_____ .

MY MOST OBVIOUS NERVOUS TIC IS:

_____

_____

_____

_____

_____

_____

_____

MY PARTNER'S MOST OBVIOUS NERVOUS TIC IS:

_____

_____

_____

_____

_____

_____

_____

MY CHILDHOOD DREAM JOB IS:

_____

_____ .

- -

MY PARTNER WANTED TO BE A

_____

_____

WHEN THEY GREW UP.

· ·

IF WE WERE TO PLAY STRIP POKER, IT WOULD BE
_____ MINUTES UNTIL I WAS COMPLETELY NAKED.

- -

MY PARTNER WOULD LAST THIS LONG: _____ .

FAITH AND RELIGION PLAY THIS ROLE IN MY LIFE:

_____

_____

_____

_____

_____

_____

_____

_____

IN MY PARTNER'S LIFE:

_____

_____

_____

_____

_____

_____

_____

_____

I IDENTIFY MOST WITH THIS CHARACTER
IN FICTION BECAUSE:

_____

_____

_____

_____

_____

_____

_____

- -

MY PARTNER IS MOST LIKE _____

IN_____ BECAUSE:

_____

_____

_____

_____

_____

_____

_____

I DEAL WITH CONFLICT RESOLUTION IN THESE WAYS:

_____

_____

_____

_____

_____

_____

_____

MY PARTNER DEALS WITH CONFLICT RESOLUTION
IN THESE WAYS:

_____

_____

_____

_____

_____

_____

_____

_____

PHYSICAL FITNESS . . .

a) Is important to me. I work out. Feel my bicep.

b) Want to go for a run?

c) I could be doing better and
want to do better.

d) My love handles have a hold on me.

- -

MY PARTNER WOULD SAY:

_____

_____

HOUSEWORK . . .

a) Let's get a maid.

b) Let's split up the work.

c) I prefer these chores:

_____

_____

_____

_____.

d) I dislike these chores:

_____

_____

_____

_____.

MY PARTNER WOULD SAY:

_____

_____

_____

_____.

WHEN I SEE _____,
IT MAKES ME ANGRY BECAUSE:

_____

_____

_____

_____

_____

_____.

- -

THIS MAKES MY PARTNER ANGRY:

_____

_____

_____

_____

_____

_____

_____.

I LIKE MYSELF MOST WHEN:

_____

_____

_____

_____

_____

_____

_____

_____ .

I LIKE MY PARTNER MOST WHEN:

_____

_____

_____

_____

_____

_____

_____

_____ .

MY FAVORITE ADOLESCENT GAME WAS:

a) Twister

b) Beer pong

c) Faking my mother's signature

d) Dungeons and Dragons

e) Other: _____

MY PARTNER'S FAVORITE ADOLESCENT GAME WAS:

_____

_____

I'M ALLERGIC TO:

_____

_____

_____

_____

_____

_____

_____

MY PARTNER IS ALLERGIC TO:

_____

_____

_____

_____

_____

_____

_____

IMPORTANT QUOTES OR ADVICE
THAT ARE IMPORTANT TO ME:

_____

_____

_____

_____

_____

_____

_____

- -

MY PARTNER ALWAYS QUOTES THIS:

_____

_____

_____

_____

_____

_____

_____

_____

I FEEL MOST LIKE MYSELF WHEN I'M WEARING:

_____

_____

_____

_____

_____

_____

_____

_____

MY PARTNER IS MOST COMFORTABLE IN:

_____

_____

_____

_____

_____

_____

_____

_____

NOISES THAT DRIVE ME UP A WALL:

_____

_____

_____

_____

_____

_____

_____

MY PARTNER HATES THESE SOUNDS:

_____

_____

_____

_____

_____

_____

_____

I LEARN BEST:

a) Visually

b) By talking and asking questions

c) By being left alone to study and stare at the incomprehensible manual

d) By doing it with my own hands, and swearing loudly, manual or not

MY PARTNER LEARNS BEST BY:

_____

_____

THIS IS HOW I TAKE CRITICISM BEST:

_____

_____

_____

_____

_____

_____

_____

MY PARTNER TAKES CRITICISM BEST IN THIS FORM:

_____

_____

_____

_____

_____

_____

_____

MY TOP 3 FAVORITE SONGS ARE, AND HERE'S WHY:

_____

_____

_____

_____

_____

_____

_____ .

MY PARTNER'S FAVORITE SONGS ARE:

_____

_____

_____

_____

_____

_____

_____ .

THESE KINDS OF THINGS ARE OK TO SHARE ON SOCIAL MEDIA. CHECK ALL THAT APPLY:

Please insert check boxes in front of each answer below.

- ❑ Relationship status
- ❑ Information about my health
- ❑ Kid photos
- ❑ Pet photos
- ❑ Saucy bathing suit photos
- ❑ I'm really private. Please post as little as possible.

- -

MY PARTNER WOULD SAY:

_____

_____

_____

_____

_____

_____

_____

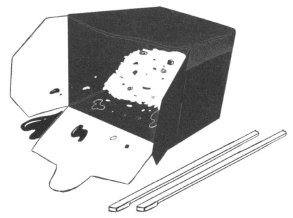

TIDINESS SCALE:

a) I iron my socks.

b) My clothes are clean and I employ the sniff test liberally.

c) My car has french fries older than me stuck between the seats.

d) There's something growing in my fridge.

e) There's definitely something growing in my fridge. It knows my first name.

f). Other: _____

MY PARTNER IS _____ ON THIS SCALE.

_____

Punctuality

IN GENERAL, I SHOW UP:

a) Early

b) On time

c) Late

d) Very late

e) I'm late for something right now.

MY PARTNER IS:

_____

_____

_____

_____

_____

_____

_____

THE EASIEST WAY TO DISTRACT ME IS:

_____

_____

_____

_____

_____

_____

_____

THE EASIEST WAY TO DISTRACT MY PARTNER IS:

_____

_____

_____

_____

_____

_____

_____

I FALL ON THIS END OF THE JEALOUSY SCALE. I THINK:

a) Jealousy is loving someone like you hate them.

b) It's only natural when someone flirts with my partner. I think they're cute too.

c) See this ring? My partner is mine forever. And then a few minutes afterward.

d) The ending of *Romeo and Juliet* seems perfectly reasonable to me.

e) Other:_____

SLEEP HABITS. I SLEEP:

a) Lava hot

b) Ice Station Zebra Cold

c) With as many covers as I can steal

MY PARTNER SLEEPS:

_____.

IT'S OK TO FART IN FRONT OF YOUR SIGNIFICANT OTHER:

a) No. Why is this even a question?

b) Let's keep the romance alive, shall we?

c) Accidents happen, and it can be funny.

d) That's love, baby!

MY PARTNER WOULD SAY:

_____

_____

_____

_____

_____

_____

_____

_____

_____

_____

_____

MY FAVORITE MOVIES ARE:

_____

_____

_____

_____

_____

_____

_____

_____ .

MY PARTNER'S FAVORITE MOVIES ARE:

_____

_____

_____

_____

_____

_____

_____ .

WHEN THIS SONG COMES ON _____,
I CHANGE IT IMMEDIATELY BECAUSE:

_____
_____
_____
_____
_____
_____
_____

- -

MY PARTNER IMMEDIATELY TURNS OFF
THIS SONG_____, BECAUSE:

_____
_____
_____
_____
_____
_____
_____

TECHNOLOGY

a) I'm an early adopter.

b) My iPhone is part of my brain.

c) I'm not tech support.

d) I'm not good at tech, at all.

e) I can work a toaster.

MY PARTNER IS _____ ON THIS QUESTION.

A MAP OF MY MIND: (LABEL AREAS BY TOPIC THAT YOU THINK ABOUT CONSTANTLY)

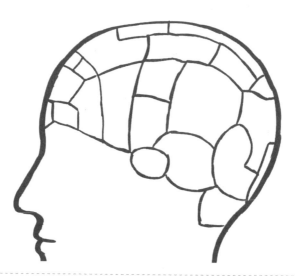

A MAP OF MY PARTNER'S MIND:

I'M MOST SCARED WHEN:

_____
_____
_____
_____
_____
_____
_____

MY PARTNER IS MOST SCARED WHEN:

_____
_____
_____
_____
_____
_____
_____

I SPEND MONEY FRIVOLOUSLY ON:

_____

_____

_____

_____

_____

_____

_____

MY PARTNER SPENDS MONEY FRIVOLOUSLY ON:

_____

_____

_____

_____

_____

_____

_____

I WILL TEAR UP AT THIS COMMERCIAL EVERY TIME:

_____

_____

_____

_____

_____

_____

_____ .

- -

MY PARTNER TEARS UP AT:

_____

_____

_____

_____

_____

_____

_____ .

MY QUIRKS ARE:

_____

_____

_____

_____

_____

_____

_____

MY PARTNER'S QUIRKS ARE:

_____

_____

_____

_____

_____

_____

_____

_____

MY FAVORITE TV SHOWS ARE:

_____

_____

_____

_____

_____

_____

_____.

MY PARTNER'S FAVORITE TV SHOWS ARE:

_____

_____

_____

_____

_____

_____

_____.

PRIVACY IS / IS NOT IMPORTANT TO ME BECAUSE:

_____

_____

_____

_____

_____

_____

_____ .

- -

MY PARTNER WOULD SAY:

_____

_____

_____

_____

_____

_____

_____ .

IF A PACKAGE SHOWS UP WITHOUT
MY NAME ON IT, I:

a) Shake it vigorously and try to guess its contents.

b) Assume it's a gift for me and treat it with respect.

c) Pretend that I hear piteous meowing coming from
   inside, and open it heroically.

HERE IS A LIST OF MY VICES:

The good

_____

_____.

The bad

_____

_____.

You decide

_____

_____.

MY PARTNER'S VICES INCLUDE:

_____

_____

_____

_____

_____

_____

_____.

CAREER-WISE, YOU'LL KNOW WHEN I'VE HIT
ROCK-BOTTOM WHEN I TAKE THIS JOB:

_____

_____

_____

_____

_____

_____

- -

MY PARTNER WOULD SAY:

_____

_____

_____

_____

_____

_____

_____

"PLEASE" AND "THANK YOU" ARE THE BEDROCK OF SOCIETY, BUT I'VE BEEN GUILTY OF THESE PUBLIC FAUX PAS:

a) Yawning openly

b) Burping

c) Blowing my nose at the table

d) Nose picking

e) Talking on my phone on public transit

f) Other: _____

MY PARTNER IS GUILTY OF THESE:

_____

_____

_____

_____

_____

_____

_____

MY PERSONAL VERSION OF THE 7 DEADLY SINS:

_____

_____

_____

_____

_____

_____

_____

_____ .

- -

MY PARTNER'S DEADLY SINS INCLUDE:

_____

_____

_____

_____

_____

_____

_____

_____ .

MY FAVORITE BOOKS ARE:

_____

_____

_____

_____

_____

_____

_____ .

MY PARTNER'S FAVORITE BOOKS ARE:

_____

_____

_____

_____

_____

_____

_____ .

WHAT MY FAVORITE MEDIA (SONGS, BOOKS, MOVIES)
SAYS ABOUT ME:

_____

_____

_____

_____

_____

_____

_____

WHAT MY PARTNER'S FAVORITE MEDIA (SONGS,
BOOKS, MOVIES) SAYS ABOUT THEM:

_____

_____

_____

_____

_____

_____

_____

HERE'S MY FAVORITE JOKE:

_____
_____
_____
_____
_____
_____
_____
_____.

- -

MY PARTNER'S FAVORITE JOKE IS:

_____
_____
_____
_____
_____
_____
_____
_____.

I FEEL MOST LOVED WHEN:

_____

_____

_____

_____

_____

_____

_____

_____ .

MY PARTNER FEELS MOST LOVED WHEN:

_____

_____

_____

_____

_____

_____

_____

_____ .

MY BEST FRIEND WOULD DESCRIBE ME AS:

_____

_____

_____

_____

_____

_____

_____ .

MY PARTNER'S BEST FRIEND WOULD
DESCRIBE THEM AS:

_____

_____

_____

_____

_____

_____

_____

_____ .

A MAP OF PLACES I'D LIKE TO VISIT:

A MAP OF PLACES MY PARTNER WOULD LIKE TO VISIT:

THE HALLOWEEN COSTUME I'VE ALWAYS WANTED TO TRY IS:

_____

- -

I'D LIKE TO SEE YOU IN THIS COSTUME:

_____

· ·

AT A CONCERT:

a) We have to wait in line before the doors open, so we can get next to the stage.

b) I'll be in the mosh pit.

c) I'll be drinking.

d) I like to socialize during the music.

e) I like to punch people who socialize.

f) I'm the come-late, leave-early type.

- -

HOW MY PARTNER RATES ON THIS SCALE:

_____

THINGS I FIND INCONSIDERATE:

_____

_____

_____

_____

_____

_____

_____

- -

THINGS MY PARTNER FINDS INCONSIDERATE:

_____

_____

_____

_____

_____

_____

_____

WHAT I MOST VALUE IN A PARTNER IS:

_____

_____

_____

_____

_____

_____

_____

- -

MY PARTNER MOST VALUES:

_____

_____

_____

_____

_____

_____

_____

_____

IF WE EVER BREAK UP, IT'LL BE BECAUSE:

a) Ryan Gosling finally returned my call.

b) Ryan Gosling finally returned your call.

c) Ryan Gosling will surely do the dishes, unlike someone I know . . .

d) Ryan Gosling filed a restraining order.

e) Other:_____

TICKLING:

a) I'm ticklish.

b) I like to be tickled.

c) Don't you dare.

d) I'm serious.

e) I'll pee on you.

HOW MY PARTNER RATES ON THIS SCALE:

_____

MY KRYPTONITE IS:

_____

_____

_____

_____

_____

_____

_____

- -

MY PARTNER'S KRYPTONITE IS:

_____

_____

_____

_____

_____

_____

_____

WHEN WE ARE LOW ON GROCERIES,
I CAN ALWAYS EAT:

_____

_____

_____

_____

_____

_____

_____

MY PARTNER CAN ALWAYS EAT:

_____

_____

_____

_____

_____

_____

_____

PUBLIC DISPLAYS OF AFFECTION RANKING SYSTEM (1-5, 1 BEING THE LOWEST COMFORT LEVEL.):

- Holding hands in the park

- Making out on the street

- Explicit trysts

- What are you doing right now?

- Other: _____

MY PARTNER WOULD RANK THESE DISPLAY THIS WAY:

_____

_____

_____

_____

_____

_____

_____

_____

I FEEL MOST AMOROUS IN THE:

a) Morning

b) Afternoon

c) Evening

d) Late night

e) What time is it right now?

MY PARTNER IS MOST AMOROUS IN THE:

_____

_____

_____

_____

_____

_____

_____

_____

_____

_____

My Sex Drive:

IN GENERAL, I WOULD LIKE TO HAVE SEX:

a) Once a month

b) Once a week

c) Twice a week

d) Three times a week

e) What time is it right now?

MY PARTNER WOULD LIKE TO HAVE SEX:

a) Once a month

b) Once a week

c) Twice a week

d) Three times a week

e) What time is it right now?

I CAN TELL WHEN MY PARTNER IS IN THE MOOD WHEN:

_____

_____

_____

_____

_____

_____

_____

MY PARTNER CAN TELL I'M IN THE MOOD WHEN:

_____

_____

_____

_____

_____

_____

_____

I'D LIKE TO TRY THIS SEXUAL ADVENTURE:

_____

_____

_____

_____

_____

_____

- -

MY PARTNER WOULD LIKE TO GIVE THIS A WHIRL:

_____

_____

_____

_____

_____

_____

**If you don't want to be explicit, use code words with an * Then use the super-secret code word page, which can be ripped out for privacy.

PRESENT COMPANY EXCLUDED, _____ IS
THE MOST IMPORTANT PERSON IN MY LIFE, BECAUSE:

_____

_____

_____

_____

_____

_____

_____ .

THE PERSON MOST IMPORTANT TO MY PARTNER,
BESIDES ME, IS:

_____

_____

_____

_____

_____

_____ .

CHILDREN ARE:

a) Our future

b) Endless joy

c) Angels on this earth

d) A necessary evil

e) No more than the transmission of genes from one generation to the next.

f) Mini-terrorists

MY PARTNER WOULD SAY:

_____

_____

_____

_____

_____

_____

_____

_____ .

I WANT TO DO THESE THINGS DIFFERENTLY
THAN MY PARENTS DID:

_____

_____

_____

_____

_____

_____.

- -

MY PARTNER WOULD SAY:

_____

_____

_____

_____

_____

_____.

I'M NEVER WITHOUT THIS (EXAMPLES: LIP BALM, SMARTPHONE):

_____

_____

_____

_____

_____

_____

_____ .

MY PARTNER IS NEVER WITHOUT:

_____

_____

_____

_____

_____

_____

_____

_____ .

SPOILERS

a) I don't care if you reveal the plot of a TV or movie.

b) I really try to avoid spoilers.

c) Spoil this show that I'm binge-watching and you are dead to me.

- -

MY PARTNER WOULD SAY:

_____

_____

_____

_____

_____

_____

_____

_____

_____

_____

_____

_____

MY FAMILY TRADITIONS INCLUDE:

_____

_____

_____

_____

_____

_____

_____

MY PARTNER'S FAMILY TRADITIONS INCLUDE:

_____

_____

_____

_____

_____

_____

_____

AT ALL TYPES OF ENTERTAINMENT, I PREFER TO SIT:

a) Close

b) On the first level

c) Near the bathroom

d) In the balcony

e) Let's stay home.

HOW MY PARTNER RATES ON THIS SCALE:

MY MOM WOULD DESCRIBE ME AS:

_____

_____

_____

_____

_____

_____

_____ .

MY PARTNER'S MOM WOULD DESCRIBE THEM AS:

_____

_____

_____

_____

_____

_____

_____ .

IMAGINATION AND SPONTANEITY ARE ESSENTIAL /
NOT ESSENTIAL IN A ROMANCE. HERE'S WHY:

_____

_____

_____

_____

_____

_____

_____.

MY PARTNER WOULD SAY THEY DEMONSTRATE
THIS BY:

_____

_____

_____

_____

_____

_____

_____.

I NEED HELP WITH:

_____

_____

_____

_____

_____

_____

_____

MY PARTNER CAN HELP ME WITH THIS BY:

_____

_____

_____

_____

_____

_____

_____

MY PARTNER STRUGGLES WITH:

_____

_____

_____

_____

_____

_____

_____ .

- -

I CAN HELP THEM BY:

_____

_____

_____

_____

_____

_____

_____

_____ .

HOW I SHOW AFFECTION:

_____

_____

_____

_____

_____

_____

_____

_____ .

- -

MY PARTNER SHOWS AFFECTION BY:

_____

_____

_____

_____

_____

_____

_____

_____ .

HOW I PREFER TO RECEIVE AFFECTION:

_____

_____

_____

_____

_____

_____

_____

HOW MY PARTNER WOULD PREFER TO RECEIVE AFFECTION:

_____

_____

_____

_____

_____

_____

_____

THESE ARE MY NON-NEGOTIABLE, ABSOLUTE
DEAL-BREAKERS THAT I CAN'T LIVE WITH:

_____

_____

_____

_____

_____

_____

_____

- -

MY PARTNER'S LIST INCLUDES:

_____

_____

_____

_____

_____

_____

_____

_____

HERE'S HOW I BEST COMMUNICATE:

_____
_____
_____
_____
_____
_____
_____
_____
_____

HOW MY PARTNER BEST COMMUNICATES:

_____
_____
_____
_____
_____
_____
_____
_____
_____

MONEY MANAGEMENT

a) My 401K is huge. I said so in my Tinder profile.

b) I'm good with money. Check out my flash roll.

c) I need to know more about retirement and savings.

d) Hey, my (vinyl collection, comic books, baseball cards) is worth thousands!

e) I've got five scratch-off lottery tickets that will take care of us both.

f) Other: _____

HOW MY PARTNER RATES ON THIS SCALE:

_____

_____

_____

_____

_____

_____

_____

MY DREAM JOB IS:

_____

_____

_____

_____

_____

_____

_____ .

MY PARTNER'S DREAM JOB IS:

_____

_____

_____

_____

_____

_____

_____ .

IF SOMEONE DESIGNED A DOWNTOWN BUILT
WITH SHOPS CATERING JUST TO ME,
IT WOULD LOOK LIKE THIS:
(label shop windows)

MY PARTNER'S DOWNTOWN LOOKS LIKE THIS:

SENSE OF HUMOR:

a) I have the go-for-the-joke gene.

b) I can't tell jokes.

c) When coached, I can tell a decent joke.

d) I laugh easily.

e) I'm a tough crowd.

HOW MY PARTNER RATES ON THIS SCALE:

I DON'T FIND _____ FUNNY, BECAUSE:

_____

_____

_____

_____

_____

_____

_____

_____ .

- -

MY PARTNER DOESN'T FIND _____
FUNNY, BECAUSE:

_____

_____

_____

_____

_____

_____

_____ .

THESE SUBJECTS MAKE ME LAUGH, DESPITE MYSELF:

_____

_____

_____

_____

_____

_____

_____

MAKES MY PARTNER LAUGH, WITHOUT FAIL.

_____

_____

_____

_____

_____

_____

_____

Food survey:

I WILL ALWAYS EAT:

_____

_____

_____

_____

_____

_____

_____

MY FAVORITE RESTAURANTS ARE:

_____

_____

_____

_____

_____

_____

_____

THIS FOOD IS AN ABOMINATION,
PLEASE DON'T ASK ME TO EAT IT:

_____

_____

_____

_____

_____

_____

_____

_____

MY PARTNER HATES THESE FOODS:

_____

_____

_____

_____

_____

_____

_____

_____

_____

I CAN'T SAY NO WHEN SOMEONE BRINGS
THIS FOOD INTO THE OFFICE:

_____

_____

_____

_____

_____

_____

MY PARTNER WOULD SAY:

_____

_____

_____

_____

_____

_____

_____

I'M STILL FRIENDS / NOT FRIENDS WITH MY EXES.
(CIRCLE ONE)

HERE'S WHY:

_____

_____

_____

_____

_____

_____

_____ .

- -

MY PARTNER IS STILL FRIENDS / NOT FRIENDS
WITH THEIR EXES BECAUSE:

_____

_____

_____

_____

_____

_____ .

YOU SHOULD KNOW THIS ABOUT
MY RELATIONSHIP WITH MY:

Father

_____

_____

_____

Mother

_____

_____

_____

Brother

_____

_____

Sister

_____

_____

I KNOW THIS ABOUT MY PARTNER'S FAMILY RELATIONSHIPS:

Father

_____

_____

_____

Mother

_____

_____

_____

Brother

_____

_____

Sister

_____

_____

WHEN WE ARGUE, WE CAN FIND MIDDLE GROUND BY:

_____

_____

_____

_____

_____

_____

_____

MY PARTNER WOULD SAY:

_____

_____

_____

_____

_____

_____

_____

_____

HERE'S HOW I DEAL WITH CHANGE:

_____

_____

_____

_____

_____

_____

_____

MY PARTNER DEALS WITH CHANGE BY:

_____

_____

_____

_____

_____

_____

_____

_____

YOU'LL KNOW THAT I'M STRESSED-OUT WHEN:

a) I'm biting my nails.

b) I'm biting your nails.

c) I'm eating ice cream out of the container.

d) I'm in the fetal position, watching reruns of "30 Rock."

e) Other:_____

_____

_____

- -

I KNOW MY PARTNER IS STRESSED-OUT WHEN:

_____

_____

_____

_____

_____

_____

_____

_____

_____

I DEAL WITH ANXIETY BEST WHEN I'M:

a) Left alone

b) Medicated

c) Exercising

d) Cuddled up with you

e) I don't have anxiety. Strong. Like bull.

f) Other:_____

_____

_____.

- -

MY PARTNER BEST MANAGES ANXIETY BY:

_____

_____

_____

_____

_____

_____

_____

_____.

HERE'S A PICTURE THAT I DREW OF US TOGETHER:

(Flip to the back of the book to see my partner's version.)

THIS BOOK IS _____% ACCURATE.

HERE'S A PICTURE THAT I DREW OF US TOGETHER:

(Flip to the back of the book to see my partner's version.)

THIS BOOK IS _____% ACCURATE.

I DEAL WITH ANXIETY BEST WHEN I'M:

a) Left alone

b) Medicated

c) Exercising

d) Cuddled up with youe) I don't have anxiety. Strong. Like bull.

f) Other:_____

_____

_____.

MY PARTNER BEST MANAGES ANXIETY BY:

_____

_____

_____

_____

_____

_____

_____

_____.

YOU'LL KNOW THAT I'M STRESSED-OUT WHEN:

a) I'm biting my nails.

b) I'm biting your nails.

c) I'm eating ice cream out of the container.

d) I'm in the fetal position, watching reruns of "30 Rock."

e) Other:_____

_____

_____.

I KNOW MY PARTNER IS STRESSED-OUT WHEN:

_____

_____

_____

_____

_____

_____

_____.

HERE'S HOW I DEAL WITH CHANGE:

_____

_____

_____

_____

_____

_____

_____

MY PARTNER DEALS WITH CHANGE BY:

_____

_____

_____

_____

_____

_____

_____

MY PARTNER WOULD SAY:

_____

_____

_____

_____

_____

_____

_____

- -

WHEN WE ARGUE, WE CAN FIND MIDDLE GROUND BY:

_____

_____

_____

_____

_____

_____

_____

I KNOW THIS ABOUT MY PARTNER'S
FAMILY RELATIONSHIPS:

Father

_____
_____

Mother

_____
_____

Brother

_____
_____

Sister

_____
_____

YOU SHOULD KNOW THIS ABOUT
MY RELATIONSHIP WITH MY:

Father

_____

_____

_____

Mother

_____

_____

_____

Brother

_____

_____

Sister

_____

_____

I'M STILL FRIENDS / NOT FRIENDS WITH MY EXES.
(CIRCLE ONE)

HERE'S WHY:

_____

_____

_____

_____

_____

_____

_____

_____

MY PARTNER IS STILL FRIENDS / NOT FRIENDS
WITH THEIR EXES BECAUSE:

_____

_____

_____

_____

_____

_____

I CAN'T SAY NO WHEN SOMEONE BRINGS
THIS FOOD INTO THE OFFICE:

_____

_____

_____

_____

_____

_____

_____

MY PARTNER WOULD SAY:

_____

_____

_____

_____

_____

_____

_____

MY PARTNER HATES THESE FOODS:

THIS FOOD IS AN ABOMINATION,
PLEASE DON'T ASK ME TO EAT IT:

Food survey:

I WILL ALWAYS EAT:

MY FAVORITE RESTAURANTS ARE:

THESE SUBJECTS MAKE ME LAUGH, DESPITE MYSELF:

_____

_____

_____

_____

_____

_____

_____

_ _

_____

_____

_____

_____

_____

_____

MAKES MY PARTNER LAUGH, WITHOUT FAIL.

I DON'T FIND _____ FUNNY, BECAUSE:

_____

_____

_____

_____

_____

_____

_____.

MY PARTNER DOESN'T FIND _____
FUNNY, BECAUSE:

_____

_____

_____

_____

_____

_____.

SENSE OF HUMOR:

      a) I have the go-for-the-joke gene.

      b) I can't tell jokes.

      c) When coached, I can tell a decent joke.

      d) I laugh easily.

      e) I'm a tough crowd.

- -

HOW MY PARTNER RATES ON THIS SCALE:

_____.

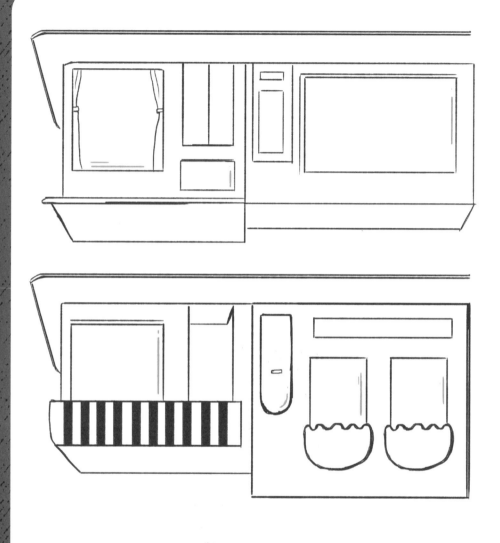

MY PARTNER'S DOWNTOWN LOOKS LIKE THIS:

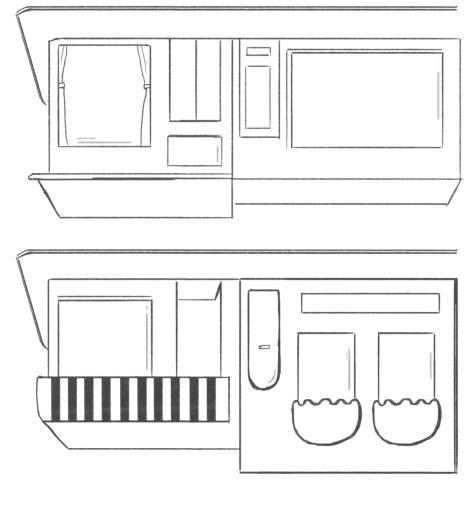

IF SOMEONE DESIGNED A DOWNTOWN BUILT
WITH SHOPS CATERING JUST TO ME,
IT WOULD LOOK LIKE THIS:

(label shop windows)

MY PARTNER'S DREAM JOB IS:

MY DREAM JOB IS:

MONEY MANAGEMENT

a) My 401K is huge. I said so in my Tinder profile.

b) I'm good with money. Check out my flash roll.

c) I need to know more about retirement and savings.

d) Hey, my (vinyl collection, comic books, baseball cards) is worth thousands!

e) I've got five scratch-off lottery tickets that will take care of us both.

f) Other: _____

HOW MY PARTNER RATES ON THIS SCALE:

_____

_____

_____

_____

_____

_____

_____

_____

HERE'S HOW I BEST COMMUNICATE:

_____

_____

_____

_____

_____

_____

_____

- -

HOW MY PARTNER BEST COMMUNICATES:

_____

_____

_____

_____

_____

_____

_____

THESE ARE MY NON-NEGOTIABLE, ABSOLUTE
DEAL-BREAKERS THAT I CAN'T LIVE WITH:

MY PARTNER'S LIST INCLUDES:

HOW I PREFER TO RECEIVE AFFECTION:

_____

_____

_____

_____

_____

_____

HOW MY PARTNER WOULD PREFER TO
RECEIVE AFFECTION:

_____

_____

_____

_____

_____

_____

MY PARTNER SHOWS AFFECTION BY:

_____

_____

_____

_____

_____

_____

_____

HOW I SHOW AFFECTION:

_____

_____

_____

_____

_____

_____

_____

MY PARTNER STRUGGLES WITH:

_____

_____

_____

_____

_____

_____

_____

I CAN HELP THEM BY:

_____

_____

_____

_____

_____

_____

_____

MY PARTNER CAN HELP ME WITH THIS BY:

I NEED HELP WITH:

IMAGINATION AND SPONTANEITY ARE ESSENTIAL /
NOT ESSENTIAL IN A ROMANCE. HERE'S WHY:

MY PARTNER WOULD SAY THEY DEMONSTRATE
THIS BY:

MY MOM WOULD DESCRIBE ME AS:

_____

_____

_____

_____

_____

_____

_____

_____

MY PARTNER'S MOM WOULD DESCRIBE THEM AS:

_____

_____

_____

_____

_____

_____

_____

AT ALL TYPES OF ENTERTAINMENT, I PREFER TO SIT:

a) Close

b) On the first level

c) Near the bathroom

d) In the balcony

e) Let's stay home.

- -

HOW MY PARTNER RATES ON THIS SCALE:

_____ .

MY PARTNER'S FAMILY TRADITIONS INCLUDE:

_____

_____

_____

_____

_____

_____

MY FAMILY TRADITIONS INCLUDE:

- -

_____

_____

_____

_____

_____

_____

SPOILERS

a) I don't care if you reveal the plot of a TV or movie.

b) I really try to avoid spoilers.

c) Spoil this show that I'm binge-watching and you are dead to me.

MY PARTNER WOULD SAY:

_____

_____

_____

_____

_____

_____

_____

_____

_____

_____

_____

MY PARTNER IS NEVER WITHOUT:

_____

I'M NEVER WITHOUT THIS (EXAMPLES: LIP BALM, SMARTPHONE):

I WANT TO DO THESE THINGS DIFFERENTLY
THAN MY PARENTS DID:

_____

_____

_____

_____

_____

MY PARTNER WOULD SAY:

_____

_____

_____

_____

_____

_____

CHILDREN ARE:

a) Our future

b) Endless joy

c) Angels on this earth

d) A necessary evil

e) No more than the transmission of genes from one generation to the next.

f) Mini-terrorists

MY PARTNER WOULD SAY:

_____

_____

_____

_____

_____

_____

_____

_____

PRESENT COMPANY EXCLUDED, _____ IS
THE MOST IMPORTANT PERSON IN MY LIFE, BECAUSE:

_____

_____

_____

_____

_____

_____

_____ .

THE PERSON MOST IMPORTANT TO MY PARTNER,
BESIDES ME, IS:

_____

_____

_____

_____

_____

_____

_____ .

I'D LIKE TO TRY THIS SEXUAL ADVENTURE:

_____
_____
_____
_____
_____
_____
_____

- -

MY PARTNER WOULD LIKE TO GIVE THIS A WHIRL:

_____
_____
_____
_____
_____
_____
_____

**If you don't want to be explicit, use code words with an * Then use the super-secret code word page, which can be ripped out for privacy.

I CAN TELL WHEN MY PARTNER IS IN THE MOOD WHEN:

_____

_____

_____

_____

_____

_____

_____

_____

MY PARTNER CAN TELL I'M IN THE MOOD WHEN:

_____

_____

_____

_____

_____

_____

_____

_____

My Sex Drive:

IN GENERAL, I WOULD LIKE TO HAVE SEX:

a) Once a month

b) Once a week

c) Twice a week

d) Three times a week

e) What time is it right now?

MY PARTNER WOULD LIKE TO HAVE SEX:

a) Once a month

b) Once a week

c) Twice a week

d) Three times a week

e) What time is it right now?

I FEEL MOST AMOROUS IN THE:

a) Morning

b) Afternoon

c) Evening

d) Late night

e) What time is it right now?

MY PARTNER IS MOST AMOROUS IN THE:

_____

_____

_____

_____

_____

_____

_____

_____

_____

_____

_____

PUBLIC DISPLAYS OF AFFECTION RANKING SYSTEM (1-5, 1 BEING THE LOWEST COMFORT LEVEL.):

- Holding hands in the park

- Making out on the street

- Explicit trysts

- What are you doing right now?

- Other: _____

MY PARTNER WOULD RANK THESE DISPLAY THIS WAY:

_____

_____

_____

_____

_____

_____

_____

_____

_____

_____ .

WHEN WE ARE LOW ON GROCERIES,
I CAN ALWAYS EAT:

_____

_____

_____

_____

_____

_____

MY PARTNER CAN ALWAYS EAT:

_____

_____

_____

_____

_____

_____

_____

MY KRYPTONITE IS:

_____
_____
_____
_____
_____
_____

MY PARTNER'S KRYPTONITE IS:

- -

_____
_____
_____
_____
_____
_____

IF WE EVER BREAK UP, IT'LL BE BECAUSE:

a) Ryan Gosling finally returned my call.

b) Ryan Gosling finally returned your call.

c) Ryan Gosling will surely do the dishes, unlike someone I know . . .

d) Ryan Gosling filed a restraining order.

e) Other:_____

TICKLING:

a) I'm ticklish.

b) I like to be tickled.

c) Don't you dare.

d) I'm serious.

e) I'll pee on you.

HOW MY PARTNER RATES ON THIS SCALE:

_____.

MY PARTNER MOST VALUES:

_____

_____

_____

_____

_____

_____

_____

- -

WHAT I MOST VALUE IN A PARTNER IS:

_____

_____

_____

_____

_____

_____

_____

THINGS MY PARTNER FINDS INCONSIDERATE:

_____
_____
_____
_____
_____
_____
_____

THINGS I FIND INCONSIDERATE:

_____
_____
_____
_____
_____
_____
_____
_____

THE HALLOWEEN COSTUME I'VE ALWAYS WANTED TO TRY IS:

_____ .

- -

I'D LIKE TO SEE YOU IN THIS COSTUME:

_____ .

• •

AT A CONCERT:

a) We have to wait in line before the doors open,
so we can get next to the stage.

b) I'll be in the mosh pit.

c) I'll be drinking.

d) I like to socialize during the music.

e) I like to punch people who socialize.

f) I'm the come-late, leave-early type.

- -

HOW MY PARTNER RATES ON THIS SCALE:

_____ .

A MAP OF PLACES MY PARTNER WOULD LIKE TO VISIT:

A MAP OF PLACES I'D LIKE TO VISIT:

MY PARTNER'S BEST FRIEND WOULD
DESCRIBE THEM AS:

_____

_____

_____

_____

_____

_____

- -

MY BEST FRIEND WOULD DESCRIBE ME AS:

_____

_____

_____

_____

_____

_____

MY PARTNER FEELS MOST LOVED WHEN:

_____

I FEEL MOST LOVED WHEN:

HERE'S MY FAVORITE JOKE:

_____

_____

_____

_____

_____

_____

_____

MY PARTNER'S FAVORITE JOKE IS:

_____

_____

_____

_____

_____

_____

_____

WHAT MY PARTNER'S FAVORITE MEDIA (SONGS, BOOKS, MOVIES) SAYS ABOUT THEM:

_____

_____

_____

_____

_____

_____

WHAT MY FAVORITE MEDIA (SONGS, BOOKS, MOVIES) SAYS ABOUT ME:

_____

_____

_____

_____

_____

_____

MY PARTNER'S FAVORITE BOOKS ARE:

MY FAVORITE BOOKS ARE:

MY PERSONAL VERSION OF THE 7 DEADLY SINS:

_____

_____

_____

_____

_____

_____

_____

MY PARTNER'S DEADLY SINS INCLUDE:

_____

_____

_____

_____

_____

_____

_____

"PLEASE" AND "THANK YOU" ARE THE BEDROCK OF
SOCIETY, BUT I'VE BEEN GUILTY OF THESE PUBLIC
FAUX PAS:

a) Yawning openly

b) Burping

c) Blowing my nose at the table

d) Nose picking

e) Talking on my phone on public transit

f) Other: _____

MY PARTNER IS GUILTY OF THESE:

_____

_____

_____

_____

_____

_____

_____

_____

CAREER-WISE, YOU'LL KNOW WHEN I'VE HIT
ROCK-BOTTOM WHEN I TAKE THIS JOB:

_____

_____

_____

_____

_____

_____

MY PARTNER WOULD SAY:

- -

_____

_____

_____

_____

_____

_____

HERE IS A LIST OF MY VICES:

The good

_____

The bad

_____

You decide

_____

MY PARTNER'S VICES INCLUDE:

_____

_____

_____

_____

_____

_____

_____

IF A PACKAGE SHOWS UP WITHOUT MY NAME ON IT, I:

a) Shake it vigorously and try to guess its contents.

b) Assume it's a gift for me and treat it with respect.

c) Pretend that I hear piteous meowing coming from inside, and open it heroically.

PRIVACY IS / IS NOT IMPORTANT TO ME BECAUSE:

_____

_____

_____

_____

_____

_____

_____

_____

MY PARTNER WOULD SAY:

_____

_____

_____

_____

_____

_____

_____

_____

MY FAVORITE TV SHOWS ARE:

MY PARTNER'S FAVORITE TV SHOWS ARE:

MY PARTNER'S QUIRKS ARE:

_____
_____
_____
_____
_____
_____

- - - - - - - - - - - - - - - - -

MY QUIRKS ARE:

_____
_____
_____
_____
_____
_____
_____

I WILL TEAR UP AT THIS COMMERCIAL EVERY TIME:

_____

_____

_____

_____

_____

_____.

MY PARTNER TEARS UP AT:

_____

_____

_____

_____

_____

_____.

MY PARTNER SPENDS MONEY FRIVOLOUSLY ON:

_____

_____

_____

_____

_____

_____

I SPEND MONEY FRIVOLOUSLY ON:

_____

_____

_____

_____

_____

_____

MY PARTNER IS MOST SCARED WHEN:

_____

_____

_____

_____

_____

_____

_____

_____

I'M MOST SCARED WHEN:

_____

_____

_____

_____

_____

_____

_____

A MAP OF MY MIND: (LABEL AREAS BY TOPIC THAT YOU THINK ABOUT CONSTANTLY)

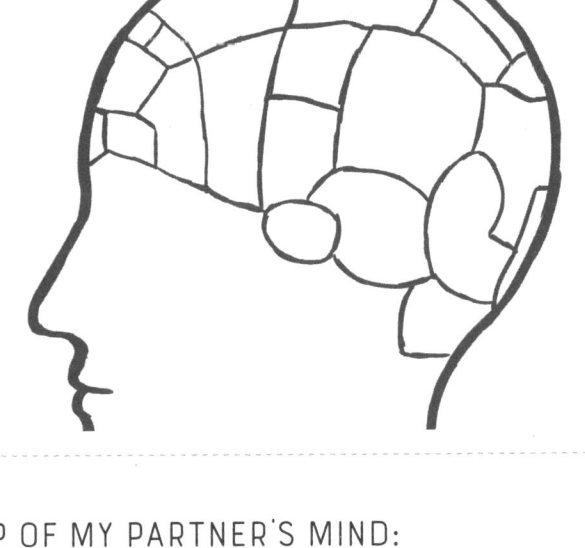

A MAP OF MY PARTNER'S MIND:

TECHNOLOGY

a) I'm an early adopter.

b) My iPhone is part of my brain.

c) I'm not tech support.

d) I'm not good at tech, at all.

e) I can work a toaster.

MY PARTNER IS _____ ON THIS QUESTION.

WHEN THIS SONG COMES ON
I CHANGE IT IMMEDIATELY BECAUSE:

MY PARTNER IMMEDIATELY TURNS OFF
THIS SONG _____, BECAUSE:

MY PARTNER'S FAVORITE MOVIES ARE:

_____

MY FAVORITE MOVIES ARE:

IT'S OK TO FART IN FRONT OF YOUR SIGNIFICANT OTHER:

a) No. Why is this even a question?

b) Let's keep the romance alive, shall we?

c) Accidents happen, and it can be funny.

d) That's love, baby!

MY PARTNER WOULD SAY:

I FALL ON THIS END OF THE JEALOUSY SCALE. I THINK:

a) Jealousy is loving someone like you hate them.

b) It's only natural when someone flirts with my partner. I think they're cute too.

c) See this ring? My partner is mine forever. And then a few minutes afterward.

d) The ending of *Romeo and Juliet* seems perfectly reasonable to me.

e) Other:_____

....

SLEEP HABITS. I SLEEP:

a) Lava hot

b) Ice Station Zebra Cold

c) With as many covers as I can steal

- -

MY PARTNER SLEEPS:

_____.

THE EASIEST WAY TO DISTRACT ME IS:

_____

_____

_____

_____

_____

_____

_____

_____

THE EASIEST WAY TO DISTRACT MY PARTNER IS:

_____

_____

_____

_____

_____

_____

_____

_____

Punctuality

IN GENERAL, I SHOW UP:

a) Early

b) On time

c) Late

d) Very late

e) I'm late for something right now.

- -

MY PARTNER IS:

_____

_____

_____

_____

_____

_____

_____

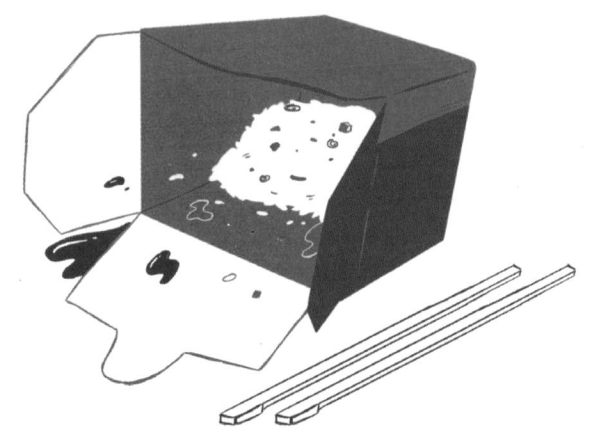

TIDINESS SCALE:

    a) I iron my socks.

    b) My clothes are clean and I employ the sniff test liberally.

    c) My car has french fries older than me stuck between the seats.

    d) There's something growing in my fridge.

    e) There's definitely something growing in my fridge. It knows my first name.

    f). Other: _____

MY PARTNER IS _____ ON THIS SCALE.

_____.

THESE KINDS OF THINGS ARE OK TO SHARE ON SOCIAL MEDIA. CHECK ALL THAT APPLY:

Please insert check boxes in front of each answer below.

- ❏ Relationship status

- ❏ Information about my health

- ❏ Kid photos

- ❏ Pet photos

- ❏ Saucy bathing suit photos

- ❏ I'm really private. Please post as little as possible.

MY PARTNER WOULD SAY:

_____

_____

_____

_____

_____

_____

_____

MY TOP 3 FAVORITE SONGS ARE, AND HERE'S WHY:

_____

_____

_____

_____

_____

_____

_____

MY PARTNER'S FAVORITE SONGS ARE:

_____

_____

_____

_____

_____

_____

_____

THIS IS HOW I TAKE CRITICISM BEST:

_____

_____

_____

_____

_____

_____

_____

_____

MY PARTNER TAKES CRITICISM BEST IN THIS FORM:

_____

_____

_____

_____

_____

_____

_____

_____

I LEARN BEST:

a) Visually

b) By talking and asking questions

c) By being left alone to study and stare at the incomprehensible manual

d) By doing it with my own hands, and swearing loudly, manual or not

MY PARTNER LEARNS BEST BY:

NOISES THAT DRIVE ME UP A WALL:

_____

_____

_____

_____

_____

_____

_____

_____

MY PARTNER HATES THESE SOUNDS:

_____

_____

_____

_____

_____

_____

_____

_____

MY PARTNER IS MOST COMFORTABLE IN:

_____

I FEEL MOST LIKE MYSELF WHEN I'M WEARING:

MY PARTNER ALWAYS QUOTES THIS:

_____

_____

_____

_____

_____

_____

IMPORTANT QUOTES OR ADVICE
THAT ARE IMPORTANT TO ME:

_____

_____

_____

_____

_____

_____

MY PARTNER IS ALLERGIC TO:

_____

I'M ALLERGIC TO:

MY FAVORITE ADOLESCENT GAME WAS:

a) Twister

b) Beer pong

c) Faking my mother's signature

d) Dungeons and Dragons

e) Other: _____

MY PARTNER'S FAVORITE ADOLESCENT GAME WAS:

_____

_____

I LIKE MY PARTNER MOST WHEN:

I LIKE MYSELF MOST WHEN:

WHEN I SEE _____,
IT MAKES ME ANGRY BECAUSE:

_____

_____

_____

_____

_____

_____.

THIS MAKES MY PARTNER ANGRY:

_____

_____

_____

_____

_____

_____

_____.

HOUSEWORK . . .

a) Let's get a maid.

b) Let's split up the work.

c) I prefer these chores:

_____

_____

_____

_____

d) I dislike these chores:

_____

_____

_____

_____

MY PARTNER WOULD SAY:

_____

_____

_____

_____

PHYSICAL FITNESS . . .

a) Is important to me. I work out. Feel my bicep.

b) Want to go for a run?

c) I could be doing better and
want to do better.

d) My love handles have a hold on me.

- -

MY PARTNER WOULD SAY:

_____

_____ .

I DEAL WITH CONFLICT RESOLUTION IN THESE WAYS:

_____

_____

_____

_____

_____

_____

- -

MY PARTNER DEALS WITH CONFLICT RESOLUTION
IN THESE WAYS:

_____

_____

_____

_____

_____

_____

_____

I IDENTIFY MOST WITH THIS CHARACTER
IN FICTION BECAUSE:

_____

_____

_____

_____

_____

_____

_____.

- -

MY PARTNER IS MOST LIKE _____

IN_____ BECAUSE:

_____

_____

_____

_____

_____

_____

_____.

FAITH AND RELIGION PLAY THIS ROLE IN MY LIFE:

_____

_____

_____

_____

_____

_____

- -

IN MY PARTNER'S LIFE:

_____

_____

_____

_____

_____

_____

_____

MY CHILDHOOD DREAM JOB IS:

_____

_____.

MY PARTNER WANTED TO BE A

_____

_____

WHEN THEY GREW UP.

IF WE WERE TO PLAY STRIP POKER, IT WOULD BE
_____ MINUTES UNTIL I WAS COMPLETELY NAKED.

MY PARTNER WOULD LAST THIS LONG: _____.

MY MOST OBVIOUS NERVOUS TIC IS:

_____

_____

_____

_____

_____

_____

_____

_____

_____ .

MY PARTNER'S MOST OBVIOUS NERVOUS TIC IS:

_____

_____

_____

_____

_____

_____

_____

_____

_____ .

MY PARTNER'S FAVORITE THING TO DO
ON A ROAD TRIP IS:

MY FAVORITE THING TO DO ON A ROAD TRIP IS:

MY PARTNER IS:

a) A Mama's boy

b) A Daddy's girl

c) An Uncle's wingman

d) The milkman's kid

e) Other: _____

MY PARTNER'S PERSONAL MOTTO IS:

MY PERSONAL MOTTO IS:

POLITICALLY, I'M _____.

Extremely Left　　　　Happily Moderate　　　　Hard-core Right

- -

MY PARTNER IS HERE [ARROW TO THE SPECTRUM].

Extremely Left　　　　Happily Moderate　　　　Hard-core Right

MY FAVORITE OUTFIT IS:

_____

_____

_____

BECAUSE:

_____

_____

_____

MY PARTNER'S FAVORITE OUTFIT IS:

_____

_____

_____

BUT THEY LOOK BEST IN:

_____

_____

_____

YOUR FIRST IMPRESSION OF ME WAS:

MY FIRST IMPRESSION OF YOU WAS:

IN HIGH SCHOOL, MY CLASSMATES
WOULD DESCRIBE ME AS:

BUT NOW I'M:

MY PARTNER WOULD SAY:

SHOULD MY PARTNER GO TO PRISON,
I WOULD WAIT FOR THEM:

a) Until they pass the first gate.

b) 1-2 years

c) 3-5 years

d) 5-10 years

e) A lifetime. Or, until they are shanked
in the cafeteria.

THESE THINGS MAKE MY PARTNER
THE MOST ANXIOUS:

THESE THINGS MAKE ME THE MOST ANXIOUS:

I CAN MAKE MY PARTNER LAUGH BY:

_____

_____

_____

_____

_____

_____

_____

MY PARTNER CAN MAKE ME LAUGH BY:

_____

_____

_____

_____

_____

_____

_____

THIS MOVIE TITLE DESCRIBES OUR LOVE-MAKING STYLE:

a) *The Fast and the Furious*

b) *True Grit*

c) *Cat on a Hot Tin Roof*

d) *Splendor in the Grass*

e) _____

MY PARTNER WOULD SAY:

_____

_____

_____

_____

_____

_____

_____

_____

_____

**If you don't want to be explicit, use code words with an * Then use the super-secret code word page, which can be ripped out for privacy.

THE CELEBRITY I MOST LOOK LIKE IS:

_____

_____ .

- -

THE CELEBRITY MY PARTNER LOOKS MOST LIKE:

_____

_____ .

IF IT WEREN'T FOR ME, YOU'D BE:

IF IT WEREN'T FOR YOU, I'D BE:

I WOULD GRADE OUR FIRST DATE WITH A: _____
HERE'S WHY:

_____
_____
_____
_____
_____

- -

MY PARTNER WOULD SAY:

_____
_____
_____
_____
_____
_____
_____
_____

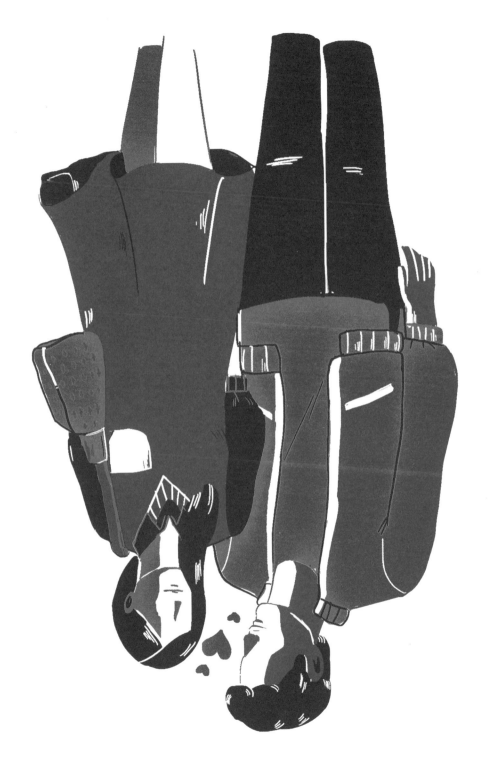

USING ROCK BANDS AS A METAPHOR, IN THIS RELATIONSHIP I'M:

a) The depraved, charismatic lead singer

b) The brooding but brilliant guitar player

c) The booze-fueled, anything-goes drummer

d) The spacey tambourine player

e) The quiet, contemplative bassist who holds everything together

MY PARTNER WOULD SAY:

SUPER-SECRET
CODE WORD PAGE

(rip out for secrecy)

really means ——————————————

really means ——————————————

really means ——————————————

really means ——————————————

SIDE B

You have reached Side B of this book. Flip it over for a full introduction, or plow ahead. Answer openly and honestly and remember that we have a tear-out code page for the smutty parts.